EVE AND HER FAILED LOVES

EVE AND HER FAILED LOVES

María del Pilar Martínez Nandín

Copyright © 2021 by María del Pilar Martínez Nandín.

All rights reserved. No part of this book may be reproduced in any form or by any electronic or mechanical means, including information storage and retrieval systems, without permission in writing from the publisher, except by reviewers, who may quote brief passages in a review.

ISBN: 978-1-956074-81-9 (Paperback Edition)
ISBN: 978-1-956074-82-6 (Hardcover Edition)
ISBN: 978-1-956074-80-2 (E-book Edition)

Book Ordering Information

Phone Number: 315 288-7939 ext. 1000 or 347-901-4920
Email: info@globalsummithouse.com
Global Summit House
www.globalsummithouse.com

Printed in the United State of America

ENDLESS STORIES

> "Adam in shadow absent of wonder,
> While Eva without you and for you,
> She keeps looking around you, her paradise."
> MARGARITA PAZ PAREDES.

MY FIRST ADAM

We lived on a ranch, we went to school together ... we met in the wheat fields, we walked quickly with my brother. We barely exchanged words but that child provoked in me ... Admiration!
He was bigger than me, dark, with a frank and strong smile, very strong ...
Once when I stumbled upon him at the edge of the canal, he hugged me so I wouldn't fall. How good I felt!
When he didn't join us on the road and skipped class, I missed him, but I knew that at night on the only street in the ranch I would see him.
It was a moonlit night, a full moon and we met to play and dance. Someone played the harmonica and pretending to be adults we danced without hugging, because according to my grandmother "To play fighting-games are a small-town sport" I never understood... what was clear to me, was that hugging was a sin, I do not know if mortal or venial did not understand the difference ... the question was not to let me grope ... How many beautiful things did I stop living by paying attention to my grandmother.
I soon stopped seeing him... at the age of 9, life changes so much...

THE RETURN OF MOM'S ADAM

That Adam was my father but I did not remember him, to tell him sweetly he was a bohemian Adam. My mother used to say that because he was a traveling agent and my grandmother more adjusted to the truth it will be… it will be… Women Agent.

One night our simple adobe house had one more inhabitant. Mom did not open the door to anyone but to that visitor yes, they talked and talked… they thought we were asleep.

Why didn't he go? It bothered me, he had all my mother's attention. I wanted to go to the bathroom and it was dark and cold I was shivering with fear of everything and the intruder. That night I wet the bed.

It took me a long time to accept that Adam in my paradise.

My grandmother was very angry with my mother and with us that we were not to blame.

With an anger that made her look ugly, she continually told me "Daughter, don't believe in men, they are the hissing snake of women, poison and more poison."

I did know hissing snakes… so it was the first metaphor that made me hate men and fear their poison.

In my innocence I did not notice the changes, but mom got fat, fat … and she suddenly was not in the house. I remember bedspreads stained with blood and the ladies of the ranch telling me … They took her seriously ill, maybe she won't come back.

God wanted her to return but these samples of the poison that put my mother on the brink of death, I lived it so many times that my legs tremble just when I remember it.

My father clouded my happy days … we moved from the ranch, he took us away from my grandmother, from the wheat fields, from my world of flowers and water, only the moon followed us but for me it no longer shone as before.

We arrived at a town, as our life improved… 57 miles separated us from my ranch and from the most beautiful grandmother, with green eyes like her walnut trees. Her advice was wise but life got tough … I stopped being a girl too soon.

My dad was more shadow than light and as a song says: It was the gray cloud that clouded my path.

MY SECOND ADAM

I was the new girl at school, I felt strange, the shy little rancher had to adapt to that different world.

I was 10 years old and I met a boy who stopped the traffic, yes! on the street from the school he was a small traffic policeman… Besides, he was the most diligent of my group.

I liked how he wore the white uniform with his Quepí … Power attracts …

Again I thought that he was going to protect me, when I came to school sad because of the violence that I lived in my house, I wanted to cry … and I dreamed that my little policeman came to rescue me, he offered me a handkerchief and I kept it to shake it, just like in the movies of the Middle Age, to say good-bye… I was his lady and he… the most audacious gentleman.

He was so courageous that he would ride his bicycle by my house every afternoon after school so I would know he missed me.

He gave me a heart of stone with our initials that I hid so that no one would ask me and discover that I had a boyfriend.

We never held hands, in fact we didn't even talk, but he wrote me little messages and he gave me his picture.

Mistake… yes, a very serious mistake to keep the photo among my books, my father discovered it … "So, you're dating, right?" This is how you pay us, we are educating you to help us with your siblings, what hope can we have if you are already crazy …

I am crazy… I thought: having a boyfriend would be bad, nobody explained to me that it would hurt my head, just in case I didn't want to be crazy and I pushed the handsome boy away from me.

I became a very serious girl, no smiles or writing notes, the poison of love should not attack my brain.

I watched Mom cry because of my father's continued jealousy and I decided that I was never going to cry for anyone.

MY BEST ADAM

I was in high school and I was still a girl, I coincided with whoever gave me his heart, but I walked away because they knew him at home and I could catch his madness.
Although it seemed that every | around me could drive me crazy, so it was better to see them from a distance.
In Spanish class we were forced to use metrics and rhyme and create our first verses.
Someone looked at me, I was nervous, I was the tallest in the class, my friends said that he was handsome, to me it was only dangerous.
One day he said some verses fulfilling the entrusted task that began like this:
Why I love you so much?
There is a beloved who asks
Your look high and sincere
A pure craving transits.
The teacher asked him what she meant by "transuta" and he replied:
-I don't know, I put it to rhyme.
We all laughed.
The most telling and exciting thing for me was when the teacher asked:
Could you tell us who inspires you?
Then the whole group started banging on the benches shouting my name.
I felt like The Dulcinea, the heroine of the movie.
He said yes, that I was, I understood it as a declaration of love.
A kind of strange love, a love of little lies, because if it were true, they would call me crazy.
Also having a boyfriend was a sin, well not so much if I did not allow him to approach me, I reinforced my protective shield

but apparently he was in love and shortened the distances, he chased me, I saw him even in the soup, he wrote my name on his tennis shoes.

Three years passed by and he did not fall out of love (or so you say it) but he went on and on, closer and closer.

We went to the state capital to finish our studies.

He was in high school and I was at La Normal, I wanted to be a teacher like my mother.

My lying boyfriend was already real, he endured another 3 years ... he was faithful to me ...

I wasn't that much, since he forgave me everything, I stood him up and ran off to the library with the least handsome boy in my group. This one, I admired him for being smart, not for being handsome. He was a shadowy Adam, he explained words and concepts to me from a book called From Paradise Lost to Paradise Regained.

I was not interested in the book, I was interested in him.

I was crazy, really crazy.

My roommates told me:

-How can you change your boyfriend for that guy? Can't you see the difference?

No, I didn't see it and I started to lose paradise.

They envied my boyfriend, a good dancer, handsome and distinguished.

He accompanied me to the graduation party, I think the cycle ended there.

In September they gave me a job and I went away, my handsome boyfriend looked for me but where I lived not even a detective would have been able to find me.

Years later when I was about to get married, he came back and told me not to do it, but...I would be crazy if I abandoned my family.

Who would help mom with the load? Now I know I was crazy not to listen to him and… I got married! … As if getting married was not for real.
I found him after many years and confessed to him in verse as his original declaration of love:

I was the crazy unconscious
That lost what she loved
For not knowing how to love….
For not understanding the secrets of the soul.

MY SHADOW ADAM

If it was not an adonis, I already told you that it was intelligent only that, although now I am convinced that not so much.

He never fought for me, although he wrote to me: "remember that in me you never die and that you will always be my sweet goddess." Where had I heard that? Sure ... my bohemian dad.

I don't know why I was lucky with poets but I didn't want to be a goddess but a loved, protected woman. I thought I would make it with him.

What a disappointment! He was fearful, he ran away from his desires, he was full of doubts, of fears, he thought that I would not be interested because my handsome boyfriend was irreplaceable, unforgettable.

I think he wanted it more than I did.

If he thought like that, what could I do to make him change his mind ... two crazy people together get nowhere.

There was chemistry, we coincided on a trip, we shared furtive kisses, it was no secret that he loved me and that I liked him, just because of that ... my dad was right, I was already crazy again.

I admired his strength, his desire to reach high and he arrived but… without me.

They all loved me very much but they married others.

He once confessed to me that I drove him crazy. I tell them that madness is contagious.

Sure, because he was crazy, he got divorced and wanted to seek comfort from me, but I was already half sane and I didn't wind up. Later I learned that he sought the company of someone very close to me and there the charm ended.

My disappointment wrote these verses:

You were not the man

You were not the port
You weren't the lighthouse, you were past!
I have not told him yet, his dark love worries me, because I am convinced that only what was not remains. I think I always looked for a father and he was like him.
There are embers, ashes of this dark love but no one can live on that, believe it or not, his gaze looks for me and attracts me but… he looks like dad… my gray cloud.
So its better to turn the page.

A TRANSITORY ADAM

Living looking for love is fun, but also very complicated.
I was excited and the bubble did not last long ... the routine breaks the pink film you imagined.
The logic for getting married that worked for me was: The chosen Adam should not look like my father.
There was an Adam who "moved the mat" but ... since he smelled of alcohol I put a mark on him, I saw that he was hiding a letter, another mark for a womanizer and I crossed it off but see ... how handsome he was!
I said this NO! I am not going to give him the pleasure of crying for him and I did not cry, I stopped him suddenly, like a medicine that does you more harm than good.
My transitory Adam looked like a movie star , he was so passionate and so dangerous that I always kept him at bay and this angered him so much that he invented a night of love that we never lived for and for which my logical Adam (my husband) suffered in silence for not daring to ask whether or not the intrigue of this spiteful was true.
This temporary love was the hissing snake of which grandmother spoke, its poison even without tasting it hurt me and there was no antidote.

THE LOGICAL ADAM

The formula for finding a husband you already know it worked.
I married the logical man, reasoning, responsible, good son, good father, excellent teacher but… but… he did not know how to love me… at least not as I wanted.
It seems that he didn't learn my name, he called me old lady on the second day, knowing that I did not like that word.
He repeated it to me so much that I believed it… Maybe that made me live with the desires off.
When I was away from my programmer, others saw me as pretty and desirable, they dared to propose that I shed my prejudices, as the song says to "let go of my hair" and thus forget the sadness and depression that haunted me.
If with these two crazy women I could not … less with the sin of deception, total madness or joke.

LATE ADAM

This man was the only one for whom I felt butterflies and heard bells.

His voice was awakening to life, working with him to find paradise.

A private paradise despite being surrounded by people.

Everything was important but more to feel it close.

He was single but I was not ... he had no chance with me ... because my wonderful children were the anchor that prevented the heart from dividing ... the mother does not leave the nest even though she cries to hold it.

I wrote him something:

Beyond your time and my time

Prisoner love stayed with me

To leave it I covered it with tears,

To live it I lacked VALUE!

We were each happy in the burning reality of marriage, when being close began

In pain I moved away forever from the wrong place and Adam at the wrong time.

I clipped my wings and went back to the old nesting box routine.

When I met with my friends, they all complained about their

husbands, I never had anything to say, never a fight, an argument, an altercation because my logical Adam said that to fight you need two and he did not enter the game.

He taught me to live with him and without him, we went nowhere together just to study in the summers.

The buildings were so far apart that no one knew that I was married.

Until one day we met in the bookstore in front of the school and (my husband) got angry for...

A PLEASANT ADAM

He was a partner, dying to make me happy. He made me laugh, he considered me pretty, intelligent and like the genie of the wonderful lamp he fulfilled my wishes.
So the summer made me want to love.
The most ephemeral love I ever lived ... My logical Adam took it out of the way, just because he was giving me the books I needed and no one should give me anything in exchange for so much attention?
I was the bone of contention, made a scandal to everyone for the only and last time.
He left me alone again and punished for being flirtatious ... I was young, not the old one he said.
The willing Adam cut a flower and gave it to me and wiped away my tears.
My young friend disappeared, he changed his career and horizons. I remembered that we had been married for two years ... of course my husband forgot and the genie in the lamp was far away.
I remember years of silence, of half words, as if we had a secret non-aggression pact of no claims.
I felt rejected, diminished, undervalued as a woman, but at least I was not crazy and I was still faithful because logic dictated that things were not so bad, they could be worse.
We were a caring couple, the couple walked, with a limp, therapy for my broken soul was imposed.
I was never aware that my wounds were not acquired in marriage, but in my childhood.
I was the girl who lacked everything who demanded more protection from her husband than passion. He wasn't strong enough to give me the one or the other.

I called him daddy and the magic for the man, for the partner, for the lover was gone.
We were friends, I admired him as a professional, I bless him as a father.
His priority was never me, but his work, his hobbies.
I'll tell you an anecdote ... once we went to a wedding of one of our friends, they all danced
I think my feet moved to the beat but my statue did not open its mouth to invite me to dance.
Someone approached me, a clueless Adam told me: "shall we danced" I was about to say yes when I remembered that I had gone with my unpleasant Adam and I told the clueless ... (sorry, I came with him) my husband didn't file a lawsuit, I think nor did he take notice.
As I longed for my best Adam, the dancer, the handsome ...
I reviewed my options, there was no more wood than what burns and I even forgot about crying.
I was not going to cry for anyone ...
I lived with my sick Adam, absent of prodigy... he was a strong spirit in such a weak body.
I think there is no worse feeling than that of pity ... he said to me:
-If you are not happy with me, leave me and move on.
And I always answered him:
-I chose you and I can't be wrong.
Without a doubt, he did not have my father's weaknesses, but neither did he have the strength and gallantry that I admired in the man who gave me life. Mom cried because she was always in love, I swore not to cry and I did not cry but maybe I did not fall in love ... I was never crazy ...
I stayed tied to what was familiar out of fear of the unknown.

There is a song that says: I am afraid of living, but I am also afraid of death
I am afraid to say that I love you and not love you and thus continue to narrate fears ...
I liked that song and a friend told me: what a negative song, it doesn't get you anywhere, I don't know why you sing it.
He was right, fear immobilizes and those fears allowed me to continue completely inert and grow old before my time.

THE DEATH OF MY MOTHER'S ADAM

He died of cirrhosis on any given day, I don't know what year... nobody told us.
He always said: "I'm going to die alone, without bothering anyone, I'm going to die far away where my love ends" (for a change, another song) and he fulfilled it ...
No one went to his funeral because we didn't find out.
My mother, when he found out, lost her will to live ... she adored him ... but also a song summed up his story.
Neither with you nor without you
Have my ills remedy
With you because you kill me
And without you, why am I dying?
I don't care about being left without a father ... although I cried under the covers and I pretended to be strong in front of Mom and said: Don't cry, Mommy, he died a long time ago, you have to bury him.

FAREWELL LETTER

Yesterday I learned where he was buried. I went to bring him a flower.
At last my heart forgave him.
Who am I to judge his life?
They say that he was never happy, like asking what he could not give us.
Now I realize that his apparently useless life had its impact on mine. He taught me nonviolence with his violence.
He taught me to persevere with his apathy, he taught me to comply with his irresponsibility.
I was everything that he was not. Thanks to the vices that he could not control, I got away from them.
With him I learned compassion, solidarity, a man so rich in talents, so strong collapsed by alcohol.
What a sad feeling of pity! I cried with him, I suffered with him and I was grateful for his abandonment.
Today without bitterness or resentment I thank God, for the father I got.
My mother does not rest beside him, that was her request out of fear of continuing to fight in the afterlife.
When I was left without the support of my mother and I felt that nothing could fill my helplessness...

ADAM WITCH

This was the most deceptive, he used many traps to get close to me, he took advantage of my depression, he made up a scientist man halo and he was just a con man.
Maybe his magic consisted of being dark, and that was the magic he used to hunt unwary women.
They were - waltz times - that's the melody that I remember as the framework of an aborted relationship.
He said he loved me like desperate, wanted sex, intense and crazy sex ... mistake ... I was not the crazy one that I seemed. I was used to the calm, the tasteless love of the comet ... I call it that because it took so long to appear ... although I recognize that when we made love, the flower of tenderness sprouted on my skin.
The sorcerer wanted to stay in my heart, I just wanted a remedy to survive through my sadness.
That dark love that wanted to stay in the shadows, did not work. His black magic didn't do the destructive effect he had planned.
I never stopped being what I was, a respectable lady and I sent him away from me.
What this rare species of man did was to make it clear to me that I didn't need sex but attention.
In the marriage therapies that my permanent Adam and I attended, we learned the technique of communication in writing.
His silences were shortened with words, I discovered that he too was a poet ... Why are the words in the verse marveling and in the action they disenchant? So much beauty was not consistent with the sad love she gave me.
Two poets together, what madness! What a soilless paradise, what an unreal sky ...

Live and compete, dream and wake up ... like spiders, each one in his thread, each one in his web. We were two parallel lines I learned to live with him and without him.

Writing serves as therapy, I have to draw out my emotions to free myself from that uncontrollable tide. In the life of every woman there are men, Adams of all kinds and "they are not lions for combat, nor are we doves for the nest" as expressed in romantic verses by S. Díaz Mirón.

My shadow Adam died, a day that I don't want to remember. While he lived I did not see time pass, when he left ... I knew that he had stolen it from me.

The years fell on me, the heart wanted to love but Who? ...

Sick NO! undecided NO! No liars, no scammers and that's what there was.

The residues of the coffee that I did not drink, of the life that was passed as a bad joke without making me laugh.

I read once that: "Love like coffee must be drunk hot."

My coffee was cold very cold, how about reheating it... It doesn't taste the same!

I was tired of warmth, of living half as well, of living for others more. I swore to enjoy the freedom. Beautiful freedom, my days for me, to touch the sky but ...

The price of freedom is loneliness, the sky disappears when there is not a star that shines for you.

All the suns were busy, when I looked at someone that little voice would appear (our operators are busy, you are very important to us, wait on the line) I told myself but ... if the least I have is time and as in politics I decided to break the online and being an independent seeker to pay for my own campaign.

I loved writing and if I found another poet... something like virtual reality.

MY SAILOR ADAM

Where do you find one of these, well in the sea, of course, I traveled to the beach ...

Do you know what? what Neruda said: "In each port a woman waits, the sailors kiss and leave, they leave a promise and never return."

My sailor was handsome, charming, I don't know if he was a poet but if he was a writer... I met him in those magical places that appear in novels, in a sunset that falls into the sea, on a path of daisies, in a courtyard of bells and trains.

He was very kind, he looked for my closeness, I saw him with a beautiful girl who I thought was his daughter, only that she seemed in love with him ... if you guessed she was his lover and he also had a wife and maybe he collected admirers, I was one of them, but his sea was not my sea and his siren songs would not bewitch me... because I plugged my ears and ran.... but as a good poet I wrote:

Tell me about the seafaring sea

But not from the water path,

Tell me about the sea that breaks

On your coasts and your beaches....

I did not see it again but I saw it in my nights full of memories ... How lucky to live it from a distance! Disappointment and doubt never bothered me. My hero was still in a display case or in a computer window, I once found that he could tell me about the skin that I do not touch about the smile that attracted him, gently to tell me that the physical does not matter but I knew that YES! my years did not allow the charm, nor the meeting.

This sailor lasted a second who was lost in his sea and to whose ports I had no access.

Today it rains, it is a sweet rain that makes me nostalgic and my soap opera heartthrob will not appear, what a blessing! I do not want to cry tears of salt, I would have liked to drown in the sea of him but it did not happen.

Where to look for another Adam, of course on the computer, I didn't have to search, he arrived alone ...

MY DIGITAL ADAM

One day there was a message for me. It simply said: Hello ... I think that in the photo he was wearing medals of those he had not collected any. I thought he's handsome and he doesn't look old, he told me in a bad translation because he didn't speak Spanish ... "I'm alone, my job doesn't allow me to relate, I saw your profile and I loved you ..." Well, two alone I think they can work ... But that "man alone" invented a place to live the rarest and most distant and most troubled in the world there in Syria, he said he was a general, on a special mission.

I who love peace, I thought: I was wrong! I can't meet him in person because he lives in the middle of a war ... Then the matter ended for me ... but ... I couldn't stop looking at his messages, partly because the translation made me laugh and it occurred to him to say nice things and flattery strange about my mouth and all the words and teeth that were in it ... but I didn't even answer him. One day he told me: "HONEY" and I let my guard down because I am sweet and compassionate too. According to my reasoning, the man died of sadness in that hostile environment that I had only observed in movies and reports ... He needed me ... How silly! I continued treating him only on Messenger but something strange happened, he never answered what I was asking him or made any comment about our talk ... well, there was no talk, but a monologue.

He said we had to get married because time was running out, will he die soon? It was the first thing that came to my mind ... will they give me a coffin and inside the boyfriend?

He called himself DESS and I started writing to him Who are you? A DESire, a DEStiny, a DEScision.

DES underlined ... He thought it was a key ... but an inner voice warned me and if it is an UNbalanced... a DISAPPOINTMENT and if it is a DISADJECT ... I think this little voice allowed me to focus more on his proposals ... The DESS was double underlined. He already had a marriage proposal and I told him that I would accept it if I knew him before. The second proposal arrived, I had to send him all my information because money is sent to a wife... YES, but I was not his wife. The unbalanced began to show ... and more when the money he wanted me to receive was to fill a room in my house, I imagined the Chinese guy from Mexico City with millions of cash ....

He kept saying that he had little time left and since the situation was difficult and the banks were not working, he would send it to me for diplomatic immunity ... I don't think he even remembered HONEY anymore and his romantic proposal only wanted my information, my identity ...

At this point he did not care about virginity, beauty, sweetness. Everything was left over, he wanted my identity.

I saw myself being persecuted by the CIA or the FBI or Interpol or, what is worse, surrounded by Mexican policemen wanting to take part of some ill-gotten money, although he insisted that it had been won by professional merit.

That virtual love turned into a BLESSING and when I was altering my life, I decided that I was stupid, stupid I was not and I did not send my data and there was no need for anything more than to block him...

He was not completely blocked, maybe Honey ended up conquering him although sometimes I think he sees me as a man ... From time to time he appears under another name, sometimes he is an oil company businessman, a diamond chain salesman, a director of a large company. But the man covered in medals I have erased ... he only existed virtually.

What a relief to get out of this sinister Adam and back to normal. A friend told me:. Eva you were curious about money, but hey, rejoice! you have one less problem ... for weeks I did not touch the computer if it were not to be the cave of Aladdin and the wonderful lamp and the character of the medals would appear to flood my house with gold.

Simple as I am I was calm until walking down the street someone yelled at me My love!

THE SIMPLE ADAM

He was not the Capitan... he was in Syria ... This was an ordinary man with a good-natured appearance, whom I had seen before ... I asked him why are you calling me my love? Do I know you? The Adam that we will call my common Adam said: I have been in love with you for a long time but you ride in a car and I walk. I never reach you ...

I tried to coincide several times (I allowed him to reach me) and talk about the simple because I am not complicated ... the circumstances were complicated, I did not know what to talk to him about, he did not invite me anywhere, I had no money and if I invited him he could be offended ...

Eva was always unlucky in extremes. One for a lot of money perhaps (Invented) another without money and this is very real, the two ADANS from the angle that you saw them were not what you dreamed of.

My Real Common Adam one day came with something for me, a watch (if it worked) and I liked the heart-shaped dial ... I was very fond of receiving his gift, he told me, you the watchband because I couldn't afford it... I remembered some verses I repeated just for myself ... "Little man, I loved you for a quarter of an hour, don't ask me for more" ...

I went on a trip alone, with his watch that reminded me that love is also a decision... I didn't see him again. Why? Life no longer allowed me to be the one that gave more in a relationship ...

Again a father to take care of ... to get out of the hole ... NO! I pass pass ... curiously the only and last gift that dad gave me was a watch. The two clocks and the two ADAMs were stopped and buried in time in the time that did not belong to me.

THE INSPECTOR ADAM

On the trip I met an Adam who we will call my inspector Adam. I wrote in a newspaper and he liked my column, he knew something about me because he had asked the editor of the newspaper ... With this Adam there were no surprises ...
He invited me to have lunch in the city where I lived, I came for him who had traveled a lot by bus. In my city there is no airport ... I noticed his tiredness, he asked me to take him to rent a car; I did it and I saw that he was walking very slow ...
I left it at his hotel, I didn't even pass, I was terrified that something would happen to him and he would see me entangled in a half romantic, half police novel ...
When I get home my daughter asks, How about your beau? As well. But ... he's old ... he's already walking slow ... Oh mommy, find yourself a younger one ... not my girl, why not? Because the young man is going to think that I am already walking slow ...
Because of that little detail, the relationship ended before it started. As they say: it was debut day and farewell ... More Adams? yes, the same, but in different circumstances.
I saw my best Adam again, I was amazed to feel that he still cared, what brought us together was a celebration of the high school generation, we had turned the clock but that night we were teenagers disturbed by hormones that I do not know why miracles flooded our bodies old.
We dared to dance and he sang Beautiful Honey... when I heard "beautiful love that God has sent for me" I woke up from my dream as a schoolgirl... someone looked at me in an ugly way... his wife! While his daughter danced with my son... What a tragedy! His time and his love of yesteryear no longer belonged to me ...

In sweet reverie I slept because the next day I would see him and the miracle happened. We were able to speak without witnesses and I am sure that: "there is always something that stays with us from so much and so much that we lose" but HE left, when I was alone, I cried, I cried... but... Why didn't I cry in time, but fifty years later? ... is something that I cannot answer ...

I wrote a poem remembering it. He sent me his verses:
To my tender friend of sweet memory
I dedicate a minute for the emotion
time has passed, memory diminishes
the more the feelings remain in the story
love story that diamonds are...

YES! for me her words are diamonds because I feel them sincere, he was always authentic, honest, the confused one was me ... I even thought I need time ... but not so many years.

The geographical distance that separates us is nothing, in time it is insurmountable....

I would like to have the magic wand and like in a movie I saw (ask the time to come back)

I'm still confused, sometimes my shadowy Adam comes to my window and I let him tell me what he never told me ... it turns out that he had to borrow words from Neruda and he wrote to me ... it is forbidden not to create your story, not to understand that life gives, it also takes it away ... not feeling that without you this world would not be the same ...

In my life this Adam was not well delineated until now when he broke his silence and took courage to tell me that if I was important to him ... I know why The Little Prince said it: "The time you lost with your rose, it makes your rose is so important ", true he dedicated minutes to me and lost years but I believe him ... for a reason that may seem trivial to them ... he sent me the John Lennon song ... Woman ... Woman in Spanish and there I understood his feelings "I never wanted to cause sadness or pain, let me tell you again and again... I love you, yes... Yes now and forever...

I hope it lasts longer than I do so that his love for me lives on... they tell me... but how else do they know who he is? What if I tell you is that I did not invent it ...

If you have read the story of my failed loves correctly, you will remember the first one they called me crazy for, the one who passed my house on a bicycle ... what I did not tell you is that he was very intelligent and was a successful doctor.

In order to love someone I need to first admire him and my admiration for this Adam was and is authentic. Just as children he sent me little letters in a pen when I found him again, we communicated by e-mail ... Sublimated love, exchange of healthy recipes, inspiring phrases and also, to vary poetry ... That is why I say that all my ADAMS loved me from afar, at a distance , but with passion not of that which overflows into beds, but of that heat that warms the soul. What else could we do but get closer through memory ...

I like the verses that he dedicated to me a little before leaving ...

I've known you a long time ago

Distracted in time, I never saw you again

Until time itself brought us together

You and me ... and clinging to time

You and me. Timeless friends we are

All the time ... just friends, you and me ...

He wrote me something about the end of his trip ... When we arrive friend, supposing that you and I arrive before the Father ... He will go first to the man and ask him: Let's see what you have in your heart? I will answer a little message for Eva ... and you, Eva, what do you carry in your heart? The little note for my Adam and two books of poems. Then I am sure that God will say: "Because you have loved ... let them pass."

His boyish love was still intact when he died. I'm sure of it, because in the last lines he wrote ... "You will always have my prayer, it won't be a big deal but prayer is the light that illuminates the path."

How lucky I am to have so much LOVE ...

Because I did not see before the love of my Adams.

Let me tell you that my logical Adam, the only one who had me in body and soul, more in body than soul, because remember that I have always been confused ...

One day he didn't pick me up at work, it was late when we went out, it was getting dark. A friend offered to take me home and on the way I saw my husband's truck parked in one of the streets ... I told my friend, get me off the car, here I stay! ...

Although she didn't want to leave me alone, she saw so much determination in me that she accepted. She was determined to find my husband. I said to myself: I have to catch him red-handed to see where he comes from and with whom. I sat down to wait. I heard music and I said it must be some canteen or a pool hall where he went.

An hour passed, two and more and he did not come out, it was like one in the morning when it occurred to me to sound the horn to beep and beep until he came out but the horn did not work, so I wanted to turn on the lights again and again but nothing neither lights nor horn ... I got down to see that the classic thing happened, it had run out of battery ...

And I thought that the inconsiderate had forgotten to come for me.

And now what could I do? It was dawn and the city looked deserted, a wrong crazy person, I was now yes ... absolutely crazy ... I walked to a taxi stand and I was lucky to get home before dawn ... There was HE who had looked for me with my mother, my friends, except with the one who could have told him where I was ...

Where do you come from? Obligatory question ... (I was sitting in your truck) ... and you think I'm going to believe you ... You're very smart how can you make up such an absurd story... Who were you hanging out with? With nobody ... And the children? You no longer have children shameless (the only insult he ever told me in his life), you are not worthy to enter this house. I was scared, his anger was against me and then my conscience shines and speaks.

I hadn't done anything wrong. Let's see, touch me, smell me! I don't come from a hotel, I don't smell like cheap soap or anything at all ... And taking advantage of the fact that the children he left with my mother were not there, he did as I told him to and he ended up making love to me desperately ... Test passed, exhaustive review and I did not fail the exam.

My teacher Adam, if he knew me, gave me joy to see that he was afraid of losing me.

I lost him first and depression took hold of me.

I felt guilty for not having given him more affection, I felt guilty for his bitterness, for his unhappiness but no ... he had in his genetics the disease that made him unhappy.

I remembered yesterday. It would be our wedding anniversary, I knew I was getting married excited, not in love. I love wearing white and wearing flowers in my hair. I was walking feeling dreamed, it was something beautiful because the people who looked at me said, It seems as if I were going to get married! That's how I felt... dressed as a bride... my tired years sprouted youth.

He was no longer there to accompany me to church but that day the bells called out our names ...

The psychologist who treated me was right when my sadness deepened and depression threatened to suffocate me.

The doctor measured my blood pressure and made me talk about HIM, and the more memories came to my mind, the more my pressure went up.

Scared, he changed his tactic and asked me to just answer him one more question ... Do you hold a grudge against your husband? I told him NOT only that I feel that all these years that I lived with him were made up of little lies... to which the doctor replied, and your children are also made up of little lies?

There as they say, I finally undersood!

I was rich with the 3 gifts my husband left me ...

I did not complain again and little by little the depression disappeared.

SILENT ADAM

One day I was traveling to a country in South America, I had to sit down with a quiet Adam, and I would have liked to start a conversation but by appearance, he was a foreigner and I deduced that he did not speak Spanish ...
I moved to another seat and entertained myself by watching the movie I chose. Beautiful movie with a very sad sad ending. I think she was French and her name was Amur... Two teachers (like my husband and I) of old age, she is ill and he takes care of her alone in their house because you know the children only get to ask, How is it going? And no one offers to take care of her. They do advise that you take her to a retirement home. The situation becomes difficult and the husband despairs, a pigeon enters the hall of the house, chases her and puts a blanket over her with the intention of drowning her ... he regrets it, takes it and lets her out through the window .... returns to the room and desperate he puts a pillow on his wife's face who already suffers too much ... I did not know if he suffocated her or frees her. Tears did not let me continue, I looked towards my seat at the quiet Adam ... and I thought I needed his hug.
"The land of tears is so mysterious" that when he saw me cry he approached me and said in perfect Spanish, is something wrong? Can I do something for you? Just hugging, I replied. That moment was wonderful ... Yes, but the magic ended because the plane was landing, I would make a stopover in Lima and he continued to another destination ...
That quiet Adam lasted in my life 3 hours ... three hours quiet and 5 minutes hugging me. Nothing is perfect!
As I got old and suffered more aches and pains I had to go to the doctor and of course there I find another Adam.

THE SICK ADAM

We had met a day before but I did not pay attention to details.

Only when he sat near me did we exchange words.

Curiously we had the same thing, tiredness, loneliness, they say: that the lack of love destroys the bones and there we were for the same reason ... osteopenia, osteoporosis, old age?

They read us the Riot Act, and we received an exercise sheet, a diet sheet… everything else… good.

To live it has been said ... Old age? I didn't want to think about it but the doctor was a geriatrician ... What I did have to think about was: how to get home? The office was in another city and I hadn't taken my car ... I told the sick Adam that he didn't look so sick, how did you get here? And he answered -in my car-. I was quick to tell him about the problem and he was very kind in offering to drive me.

I considered him my hero at that time he was the most important person to me ...

On the way we talked about everything, more me than him, he is a professional, a retired engineer and we have a lot in common, alone due to different circumstances, lacking affection and talking about the beautiful youth and the wonderful time that we had to live ... we arrived at where should I drop off.

I entered the church to thank the health that still accompanies me and I remembered what my hero Adam said to me "you pray for me" he left me his phone number, it makes me want to talk to him to say: I did it, are you okay?

You will see that I am afraid of loss and with pain the expression of my husband came to my mind in the last moments of life that we share. The last thing he said to me: "Put your hand on my head and pray for me ..."

I would like to continue in the red car of the engineer Adam. I think we need each other… can I propose? He would not dare and if I try? ... But that will be another story that I will tell you.

If we get to the next consultation ... or the next life, if there is a cyber in heaven, I will send you the end of the story.

POWERFUL ADAM

Why do I like men of power so much? I will say something about the powerful man who wanted me for himself ...
Eva, with the image of a simple and good teacher, conquered him. The mature Adam was on a political tour.
With her almost childish way of being, she got on the platform where the character was to request a nursery and kindergarten for the neighborhood where she worked.
He said yes and against everything expected of a politician, he acted quickly and made my proposal come true on behalf of all mothers with small children.
Eva read what fell into her hands and by chance she had a copy of Grandmother's House written by the mighty Adam, perhaps only I had read it, because it was not a bestseller. I think I liked him more for reading it and also for "intelligent"... I have already told you that silly, what is called silly, I was not... With this Adam I was... his sympathy for me led me to a government position in the city ... and he wanted me to go to the capital, he wanted me close ... what for? I never knew ... (I never had his time and his skin was a brat) sorry ... I heard a song. I sensed that the powerful Adam what he wanted was to file me on the list of his conquests ... They say that if I had agreed to go to his country house, I would have collected centenarians (gold coins) from the bottom of the pool. Yes, but ... What would he ask me at the pool?
Travel, gifts, land, jewelry, everything would have given me if I accepted his crazy love ...
But I dedicated myself to hide, to avoid him, to remain in my lost school among my children ... and you know what? Nothing happened, how boring you will say! Well, yes... I can't tell you about the kiss, or the secret date, or the night of passion, the man

was no longer there for that and my fears became acute. What if he dared? What if he had a heart attack in the middle of an idyll? ... This had already happened at least in the novels that I read.

I admired him, I admired him a lot, he transformed what he touched, he remodeled the entire state, he walked leaving works and he had many followers, but also many envious ones in the high levels of government.

Circumstances took him away from my life, my teacher of Mexican Literature, Secretary of Culture of my powerful Adam, told me how the networks were woven to overthrow him.

Chronicle of an Infamy, another of his books gives details that I will not tell you because it is not my intention to make a historical novel, but rather a catalog of my failed loves.

REMEMBERING MY BEST ADAM

I went to Saltillo, to my favorite place and there in front of the steps of La Normal de Profesores I thought of my best Adam, the one who was always waiting for me at the school exit door, he never missed the appointment with his sky blue shirt, I distinguished my beau from the window of the psychology room.

My roommate told me: he doesn't miss your appointments, but he misses school, he will fail the school year.

And so it was ... I felt guilty and it was indirectly, because he confessed to me that he had failed to stay another year in the capital until I finished my degree ...

While this romance lasted, he was my most innocent love ... he gave me gardenias, invited me to the movies when he could and to have ice cream when we had a peso to spare.

That day it was raining, everything looked sweet, melancholic, it made us want to walk embraced without letting go. In the air, the smell of wet earth and a sunless afternoon that announced the night.

Afternoon of youth, funny madness of two teenagers walking in the rain and counting the trees in the mall, we never knew how many there were, we did not care if, finding our tree, and the bench of the first kiss and finding the gardenia seller.

No, my Adam will not come today ... as if to make contact with the absent boyfriend, I wrote him in verse ...

Our tree no longer exists ...
Nor the gardenia seller,
Neither the ice cream parlor, nor the coat ...
Our story ... does not open ..
The key ... the key ... stayed with you ...

Echoing my call, without having to wait for the postman, at the speed of light he answered me ... the magic of the cell phone and even more so when I am thinking about it.

I read, excited. Eva ... there are things that neither time nor distance can destroy. The only thing they achieve perhaps is to reduce the intensity. I confess that the 3 years spent in Saltillo with you are my most beautiful memories. You painted everything in colors and pushed away discouragement and depression.

Today that I walk slowly I think ... I can limp on one foot, but not with my soul.

I have those experiences, of those 3 years when the world was ours. Where will the memories go Where will the dreams go?

I said to myself: -They are here, with me and in these beautiful places that one day they saw us pass-.

I longed for his hug, but what had I been to the capital for?

I tell you ... I forget everything! I need a doctor.

MY DOCTOR ADAM

Again, pretty, but if you have nothing, you are healthier than me and many-
Oh doctor, everything hurts and my heart hurts more ... Seek to be distracted ... it will do you good to walk, read, fall in love.
-I will introduce you to some friends-... and I will put an ad in the newspaper, I said jokingly...
On the internet, many gallants are advertised, but I swear to you there are no good references, the candidate I chose What a disappointment! How good that I realized in time.
I like this doctor and when I came in he gave me a kiss, he is athletic and very dark, he is from Cuba.
He reminded me of the verses of Nicolás Guillen and Martí ... I imagine him writing on my death certificate "They say he died of cold, I know she died of love."
A long time ago my doctor Adam when I had a husband and the doctor was closer because of our work, he told me taking advantage of the fact that we were alone -Eva, there are women who were not born for only one man- And that's good as long as she is not his, right?
On another occasion when the office was dark, he told me to open the curtains,
I did it and at that moment the light came back and he gave me the order -Close the curtains please-, guessing his intentions, I replied: And what flavor would you like your ice cream? I left not only the office, but work ... I was a difficult Eve ... but my doctor Adam lasted as long as a consultation and a goodbye kiss ...

THE ADAM OF THE CANE

Falling in love, falling in love again was the watchword.

I went on a trip with a group of friends to a beautiful walled city, bathed by the sea.

What a pleasant stay, I liked to walk along the boardwalk and sit next to the bride from the sea to see if the beloved would arrive on the next boat ... he never appeared.

The penalties with bread are less, we walked to the hotel and already settled in the dining room I saw that a few meters away a cane fell, I got up to hand it over to the owner who I imagined elderly, disabled, but… no! To my surprise the owner was a strong man and he was with a group of friends who celebrated my kindness.

I forgot the incident, but I always saw the owner of the cane in the same place, as if waiting for someone. A girlfriend? A wife? No, no woman accompanied him. One day I talk to a young man, I assumed it would be the son.

He smiled at me, he always smiled at me, his loneliness attracted me and I think he liked mine ...

Once he paid my bill, I was amazed that he hardly thought about him and showed up.

Of course he was not passing through the hotel, he lived there.

I went to buy a gift, he was the owner of the souvenir shop.

I conquered this Adam that I will call the Adam of the stick from afar, and his smile invited me to meet him.

He was single, he had dedicated his life to educating his nephews and he forgot to live his.

He gave me tenderness the story of him seemed that fate finally put a candidate to alleviate my loneliness.

He asked me out, but tonight… we would go somewhere else, and I couldn't accept his invitation.

The bus arrived for the group at the scheduled time and He was looking for me, a colleague who noticed this told me: Don't be bad, say goodbye, you can see that the man is sad.

I went downstairs, gave him a hug, I gave him my book of poems, we made no promises for what? Neither he would leave his life nor I mine. Now I think I should have asked him. Again, I ran to love. No one was expecting me at home ... well yes ... a faithful Adam. We will call him the young Adam ...

THE YOUNG ADAM

It is strong and does the heaviest jobs in my studio.
The floors are shiny and everything is in perfect order.
I arrive and he asks me, Are you tired of driving? Can I help you carrying paintings or books?
Always cheerful, always helpful ... I remembered María Félix that she had such an Adam ...
How fortunate that this Adam takes care of my goods and takes care of me ...
He looks happy to see me, he senses when something happens to me or when sadness or depression overwhelms me.
One day I tripped, I dislocated my ankle and the solicitous offered to rub me. His massage tasted so good, all I needed it ... I wanted more and more, but ...
You know I was ashamed of my skin, my years and my desires.
I put my thoughts in order, I saw the sparkle in his eyes and asked him for a glass of water, I pushed him away so as not to get lost in an uncomfortable situation ... I took a deep breath ... I knew that Adam required him more as my assistant than as a trivial adventure ...
For many days I did not go to the studio... the balance improved in my leg and inside ...
Surely, I was wrong seeing what he was not ... in my young Adam, he behaves in the most natural way and that pleases me ... I still avoid being close to him.

MY LAWYER ADAM

I began to answer the letters of my lawyer Adam ...
I met him in high school, I had to consult some legal details and only in him could I trust.
Miles separated me from his office, I made the trip, I was not sure what it would be like now, but I knew he was not married ... he offered me his house, I preferred to see him in another place.
I remembered Facundo Cabral "We are born to meet, life is the art of encounters".
My lawyer Adán sent me hugs at the speed of light of course on the computer.
He also wrote in a newspaper and thought that his writings and his emails were soporific ...
Very well-educated, very sure of himself, an extraordinary specimen, an honest lawyer.
I confess that sometimes I had to use the dictionary to understand its terms ...
See something he wrote to me:
Undaunted woman
only sentimental
generous and abysmal
winged to love
skillful in disappearing ...
This Adam arranged everything I asked for, he has my gratitude, we are great friends but my heart is still lethargic, lonely and worst of all with fear.
They say that only one thing makes the dream impossible and that is the fear of failure.
What an irony, two achievers fleeing love.

He is still in his office, I'm still in my studio and sometimes I read and answer his emails.

I have always put distances it seems that Eva does not know how to relate.

I go to places where there are Adams, good candidates, who could be by my side if I wanted.

I think I was born to be lonely. A flower that does not want to be cut, that has roots deep in the ground, in her garden, surrounded by high walls so that no one comes near.

I go in the wind and the dream to look for another Adam ... I find him, I will call him ...

THE MASTER ADAM

I saw him once, only once, he was treated like a special character and he was accompanied by an eccentric woman.
He wore shorts and a washed-out shirt looked like a young man's outfit on an old body ... well it wasn't the outfit; He was an old young man ... I liked that and even more his gaze fixed on me when he had to go to the stage to say my verses ... I saw something in that nervous and impatient Eva ...
I never asked him. I knew he was a great writer but I didn't ask anything... I forgot.
One day someone appeared on my computer screen that I thought I recognized.
I wrote down a comment on the subject, my opinion on beauty in poetry.
I'm not a beginner at this, but I didn't think HE saw any qualities in me. He answered my comment.
Without identifying it at all, I began to follow him, souls are better when there are distances between bodies ...
Distances in time, distances in geography, did not prevent me from being interested in this master Adam.
I found in his writings the trace of a very important woman in her life ... I wished I had been loved like that. This relationship is full of magic, it does not require a greeting, a detail, a hug, but it lives, it feeds on words ...
I learn new terms, new metrics, other styles and their joys and disappointments I make them mine ... sometimes I hear his voice in a video, I like to read it because I understand it, because when I read it I find myself ... He only answers: (Sometimes it's easy to understand each other ... Let's have a toast woman to life ... We will go where the wind takes us)

We don't need to make appointments, I find him at midnight, at noon, in the middle of dreams.

He accompanies me in my sadness and makes my loneliness light. This Adam is perfect. He does not know that he fills my life so much, as it is immaterial, he will not leave and if he does I will be the owner of his past, I will look for him in the future ... I will not mourn his departure and if one day we coincide and he does not look at me, his indifference won't cause me pain.

I will have no memories of caresses or shared moonlit nights, so again I will not cry for the man I now fully enjoy.

I saw a movie "The Remains of the Day" and in it I discovered that I want to experience the remainder of my day.

ADAM MILITARY

The uniforms have a fascination for me, those worn by the military, kings, priests ...
A military Adam has written to me and I will tell you about his proposal ... I wish a long and lasting friendship with you. Since I saw your photo I can't stop thinking of you, I'm an American, I live in Afghanistan, I'm on an important mission, I'll soon return to the United States and I want to marry you.
Tell me all about yourself... Blah blah blah, he didn't translate well but it sounded pretty suspicious to me.
Another military man only Mexican, less credible than the first. He writes to me. Hello girl and he draws a lot of kisses... It makes me laugh, I replied... Do I know you from somewhere? And he says to me: "You don't know me... So Bye. Bye Bye. Good riddance..."And this military man whose uniform was too big for him sent me a crying monkey emoji...
How well I did to block one for a suspect and the other for a crybaby ...
I do not think that in the remainder of the day I will find a king Adam but if that happens I will also tell you.

MY FORBIDDEN ADAM

Forbidden to prohibit, even so, being so liberal, this option, I did not apply it.

This man who winked at me, who got nervous, who gave me an anthology hug that made me feel like he was still alive ... is forbidden for me.

I know where to find him, at what time, how he will be dressed and even what he will say.

I have stopped confessing, I don't want him to know me, I think he likes my voice.

I can say that I like the image he projects, a mature, cultured man with years of experience in his particular mission.

I think we could talk about so many topics, I see in him a rebellious man, with new and dangerous ideas.

Sometimes I require his embrace, his comfort, his blessing ... I go over and step back ...

I can't do anything, we are two paths that will never meet.

I observe him from afar, one day I noticed that he seemed to be ill. I would have liked to make him some tea, tell him not to work so hard, that he needs to sleep well.

We all... I think... I need caresses, it was my desire to pass my hand over his forehead, to tangle my fingers in his hair... I rubbed my eyes. I came back to reality! The church wasn't a place to be thinking about that.

What a shame... I liked the priest! In that cassock I distinguished the man, he was the one who awakened my longings and desires ... What if he liked me too? Why did he get nervous when he saw me? That hug he gave me, that hug I can't forget. It lasted a long time ...

Like I want to stop for an eternity.

I thought of his commitment, of his vows and I left before the end of the mass ...

I didn't tell him anything, I'll never tell him that I wanted him in my bed.

My little devil told me ... you can look for another church, you will find ministers who get married ...

No thanks... I wanted the forbidden one!

Solution: I directed my steps to another chapel where the oldest of the priests officiated ...

I am afraid to love well and now even to leave and more to open my mouth to give my opinion.

NARCISSIST ADAM

These are difficult times and I feel like Anne Frank imprisoned in her refuge because there is a Hitlerian madman very geographically close to me ... across the river, I am terrified that when exercising his mandate as president of the most powerful country in the world he will order that we all put ourselves in row and tighten a control of nuclear weapons that we disappear. He seems to hate us ...

There is no one who loves this narcissistic Adam but he loves himself tons, he plays at being omnipresent, omniscient, omnipotent ... I think he doesn't even sleep and is not sick of anything.

To think that death could do us the favor of removing it from our space.

I am terrified that I diverted the water from the river that feeds us, that the air we breathe takes away from us and the Chinese wall of it takes us away from the family that remains on the other side. It saddens me that he is part of this generation, of which I am proud, we created such a perfect world and now a perfect idiot thinks only of destroying, threatening ... every day he comes up with a new strategy so as not to stop being news.

I would like to be a fly to enter his house and find out how Eva treats him because among all the Eves in the world I don't think there is one who can bear it.

MY SPY ADAM

I went on a trip claiming that I had to celebrate the celebrations of a movement to which I belong, as it is a women's movement, I did not think that I could find another Adam, but yes, there was one, I do not even know how it came to our table.

The poet Eva that I am was involved in her game ... a jury would decide if my material was the winner of a contest, I didn't win anything, but that night I was extremely happy.

The man sitting across from me became interested in what I was doing and we talked about my world and his. Poetry united us so much, that we did not realize that we were excluding others from the conversation.

My interlocutor knew so much that I began to admire him and admiration is the principle of love ...

Falling in love at this point in my life, seemed laughable ... I remembered a movie called "Learning to live" where the protagonist is a nice old woman with whom a crazy young man falls in love, because with her experience she took him to a world of new sensations and emotions ... The gallant was very young for me, but he had so much information about unknown people and worlds that I thought. Where will he get it from? I deduced it was a SPY.

But why was he interested in me? Of course! I could give him clues to a past more past than his and that undoubtedly kept secrets that he wanted to reveal ... maybe he was making a book and he found a source in me.

Very affectionate and attentive, he filled in details those days that we shared ...

I looked for him with my eyes, he was always with a beautiful lady (his mother) taking photos and he promised to send them to me...

for some reason he was looking for my company, but ... questions about my country? and a past not so different from the present, because it is true that I'm older than him, but I am not a mummy from ancient Egypt.

My happiness was immense when he clarified my doubts, answered my questions with precision and a reasoning so well argued that I was caught in an invisible network from which I did not want to escape.

The event where I met him was multinational, there were representatives from different countries and I saw him exchange phrases with one and the other, but he did not dedicate as much time to anyone, as he did to me... Well, there was someone he never left alone, his mother... Was he looking for another mother in Eve?

He investigated me and I also investigated Him, I will not say what I discovered, my rising love that, if it was real, collided with a wall of ice and it froze.

I ran out of wings, I found my answers and I sincerely hope he finds his own.

INDIGENOUS ADAM

What can I tell you about a new Adam, only that he is an old Adam, he still casts a shadow, I can still lean on him, maybe he invites me to the movies and we can string together memories but I'm not there, the present has no memories, the past does, and His are a very heavy burden that I cannot and am not even willing to try to erase ... The Adams who are left without their Eve feel lost and I prefer to get lost alone on the road than to be a guide.
I don't know if the new candidate will have Eva is virtual ... he makes me happy, he tells me jokes.
I think he likes beer because he says that even in his sleep he can't shake off that temptation to drink. Alcoholics no ... with my father I had to hate them.
He told me that if I invited him a beer, I told him: sleep ... so you can dream ... Could you come with me? To sleep NO! I sleep alone and you will see what beautiful dreams I have ... This is how my books were born ...
We pause the chat and then he is interested in my books ... I hope he buys them.
He says that he too wanted to be a writer. I tell him that it is still time for him to try ... and he sends me verses from my favorite poet, I appreciate the detail and I fall asleep ... he is interested in my life well, he will pass ....
I think I am no longer for Adams but I want to be loved, to get excited again.
A friend invites me to visit other places, other people, but I have already tried everything and it doesn't work ...
More by force than desire I accompany her to meet the new beau. I liked the tour, we would go to the step of the eagles, we rested next to a placid lake, where the reeds marked the shore, some

ducks were looking for food. The song of the birds filled the atmosphere and children played with a colored ball that the wind snatched away from them ... The night was filled with stars, they did not want to sleep and less with the illusion of meeting the new Adam. I saw the water shake, stirred by the wind, that's how I trembled with fear, afraid that the friend who was taking me to a new experience, will leave me abandoned in the middle of the path ... and I without a car depending on her decisions ... when she knew the way she would come alone... because only I understand myself, because I have difficulty accepting suggestions and following in someone else's footsteps. They can take away everything but my ability to decide.

If I met the gallant, I was impressed by his strength, his gallantry, his house was a fortress, for me an enchanted castle and HE, the most enigmatic prince, will call him the Indian Adam.

That Indian became a secret love ... I told my friend that I did not like him so that she would not accompany me to see him, I walked the road alone, many times ... I keep doing it, I like our encounters, I stop in front of the lake and I walk followed by the ducks, I long for the sunrise and sit on a hidden bench to have a coffee and my favorite cookies.

I confess that reality sometimes falls on me and prevents me from enjoying it ... Trip to the capital, I couldn't take it but I remembered it every moment. I entered a stately building that houses an elegant café where the best of society meets... It was full, I longed for the solitude of my bench and my simple lake coffee. They kindly found me a place in a smaller room with leather swivel chairs, in front of a bar... excellent service and tasty coffee.

Busy with my agenda in what I should solve in the big city, I turned towards the door and a woman who was heading to the bar caught my attention ... she was dressed elegantly, all in red, in her blonde hair streaks of the vibrant color stood out, lady of advanced age, still agile and upright, he came to occupy a place next to me ... Her distinguished appearance contrasted with the bad smell she gave off, it seemed that she had not bathed in months ... people changed places, I did the same because the urine odor was unbearable.

Only a man with a brand suit, white hair and an indecipherable smile remained in her place next to her, who seemed to speak alone, at least he saw her move her lips, although her voice was inaudible. Who were this Eve and this Adam? I did not know, but something united them, sometimes she would caress the gentleman's leg with her jeweled hand and he would not withdraw it ... They would be eternal boyfriends going faithful to a date in the same place and at the same time. Maybe they no longer remembered, they no longer smelled, they no longer felt, they could no longer love ... but they kept looking for each other.

I thought about my Indio and it made me want to run to look for him, before time turn me into the woman in the red dress ... How shocking it was for me to meet her, she was worthy of being a soap opera heroine but I didn't have time to investigate her life and I was left with only one piece of information. When paying the bill, the girl who attended me told me: Excuse me, we know the problem that our client causes, they all move away when he arrives, but we cannot deny him the service ... She is a wealthy person, of ancestry, but we do not know more ...

The lady was still sitting, wanting to talk with her, but she had been left in another time perhaps without memories and the same thing seemed to happen to the gallant, he left her first... Why did he leave her alone? I thought ... but she had arrived alone and she didn't feel like leaving or maybe she wasn't sure where to go, where she belonged ... Would someone be waiting for her outside? I don't know. I deduced that her love kept her standing ... it hurt me to think ... What life weighs when it lasts so long!

It was clear to me that I had to stay in love, excited, my addiction to the love of the Indian Adam had to remain to keep me agile and lucid.

I remembered his castle, his attentions, he guessed my thoughts and everything came to my hands, drink, food, fun, and his multiple servants attended me as queen.

I let go of my fears and accepted new challenges, traveling miles to see him, to fill my senses with exhausting nights of Apache love.

That enslaving relationship filled me with fantasy, suddenly I was in Paris, fortune opened its doors for me in China, fairies put themselves at my service to make me happy and dragons and whales and mysterious gifts kept me from falling asleep, also because of the gigantic hamburgers that I ate and the little devils that tempted me not to leave my lover's castle.

What a great gift life gave me, I began to love everything, to live fully, to know abundance, to laugh at the simple, to discover what is behind things, to play as if I were a girl, to seek company, to wait looking forward to Friday to see it... Today is Friday.

I ran to get my suitcase, I put the essentials in it, I would like to live in the castle of my Indian Adam but it is my secret, it cannot become reality.

I was determined that my love would last, I was not going to think about my years or my fatigue. That's how he loved me ... I tried to fix myself a bit, female flirtation does not leave me. No dark or gray clothing, bright, vibrant colors, but He doesn't like me to attract attention.

Either way, I dressed for HIM, along the way he sang, the sky was bluer. Wild flowers brightened the road and a gentle rain followed me. She listened to love songs and I had a silly smile ... What it is to be excited!

I arrived earlier than usual. I would wait for him until dawn, I had not walked so much to return without his caresses ... I felt cold, distant, busy with his business and problems ... I forgot mine and continued to admire his strategies to conquer me.

He promised me a luxury car and money to travel and see the world ... My inner voice told me ... He promises that to everyone ... but you don't pay attention to reason, well they say that: The heart has its reasons that reason ignores ... every day more in love and dependent on him.

I needed him to breathe, when the atmosphere became rarefied I would leave the castle and walk by the lake, the princess needed a bit of the moon and a lot of solitude, secluded in my room, erotic games were my lifeline to make up for his absence ... It was so cold that my bones hurt, I covered myself with the shawl, I did not look at the old woman who was reflecting in the mirror and I started to narrate what filled those moments ...

I wrote to him, without sender without addressee the pen express my truth ...

I want to be alone
sweeten the air with my soul
strip me of everything that hurts
and thus in freedom dream that I love you, without loving you ...
It was dawn, the sun invited us to adventure and to look for him again, I would settle for half an hour, to see him from afar, but I knew that falling into his arms I would renounce everything, without pride without will. Who was I?

I concluded justifying myself I am ALIVE ...
I love life,
I give up killing on me

what's good.
I give up living in a vacuum
my land is lavish and it still gives if I ask it ...
Everything was the color that I wanted to see and sadly, I said goodbye to my beloved promising to RETURN.
I am reluctant to return as I promised my Adam, but Friday is approaching and I am filled with anxiety to go to meet him ... I dream of his heart, a large heart that asks me to touch it, I hear its beat, I put my hand on it, Its rhythm accelerates and my rhythm, its light fills me, increases in intensity, when I think I reach glory it returns me to the starting point, sad reality, the sweet prize of love does not arrive.
I did not know he was so passionate, so vehement, I hide in the corners to avoid the memory of him. Change of place, landscape, environment, friends but nothing excites me, no one can take their place. Am I going crazy? They always told me that love was crazy. Crazy or not, Friday awaits me ... Will I go?
It seems that I hear the voice of my mother, my grandmother ... "don't trust men, don't be silly."
It seems that I have my logical Adam close to me again. Life is not ha, ha, learn to give up, accept that the fun is over and the obligation remains ... How many times have I cut my wings and returned to the routine of the sad nest! But no, not now, I won't do it again.
I reaffirm my decision to love and turn up the volume of the song ... "I forgot to live the small details."
The voices of my programmers are not so important, physically they are gone, but the ones that are friends and relatives harass me with their chant ... Eva is going to go wrong with HIM, he does not look for you because of your pretty face, or because of a youth that you no longer have, he wants you for your money....

My money, I had not thought about that ... what is money for but to spend it and besides if I could not buy health, I would buy pleasure, I would spend my time and my money ... Will I go?

Yes ... back on the road, with this crazy desire to love, exposing myself to everything, listening to my favorite songs, forgetting my pain, my anguish. Savoring my loneliness ...

An hour crossing bridges, hoping that on the way I have no setbacks that it takes me to my prince's castle.

I have reached the lake, on my way to the jetty, I had never contemplated the movement of the waves, for seconds I feel dizzy, trapped in that changing surface, I don't want to sink into its waters, I remembered Alfonsina disappearing into the sea and it scared me.

I was hungry, maybe that's why the dizziness was because of that, the beauty of the lake attracted me so much that thinking about eating made me feel unromantic ... but it was my reality.

The dining room door is open, I hear a voice calling me... it wasn't HIM.

A smiling young woman invites me to sit down and share lunch. Who are you? I have never seen you ... -I'm the owner's friend's wife. They went hunting. They will take some time to arrive.

I was glad to be able to chat with someone who surely knows my Adam ..

-This man is a bit strange, he gave my husband a great gift, a collector's car and he has more at the entrance -Did you notice? - No! I replied ... but a little light of hope shone within me ... for sure it will surprise me.

We continued talking trivialities I did not dare to ask a key question for me Was he GAY? I was not going to bother or offend her ... while she was resting I went to talk with the farm animals, the dragons that came out of the Chinese music box ... and some rare coins with the legend of good luck.

Time flew by, in the castle there are no clocks but I saw god Cronos staring at me, I couldn't hold its gaze, I deduced that I was too tired to keep waiting for him to arrive.

I went out to get some fresh air, the night was already falling on that lonely field ... HE didn't show up.

Once again to sleep alone and fantasize of his touch and affection which took me to the climax.... I thought ... I have pride, I will go away and I will not see him again, it is more what I suffer than what I enjoy.

At night my pains increased, it was cold, it was loneliness, it was the years that weighed down and I did not want to admit ... My heart does not get old I repeated myself and at least in my dreams I recovered youth ... I gave the reason to the one who sang ... I'm going to draw youth from my past "as if it were a bank account.

At dawn I appreciated the restful sleep and guess what? Again I went looking for him ...

I looked like a teenager ... What love makes you do! I was ALIVE and I was losing sense of reality , and I was losing my health and money, nothing mattered.

I am exhausted, I could not get out of bed, my movement is limited, each step costs me too much ... I want to cry ... Will I have more opportunities to live this crazy love?

They have denied me permission , they have hidden the keys from me but He will look for me, I am sure that we will meet again ...

They have advised me to change him for another one and I agree "Taste lies in variety".

I have stopped going to his house, I have changed the course of my steps.

I always find someone who invites me to have fun, I get tired of the game of pleasing the one at the moment.

Why do I keep thinking about the other? This one offers more. But feelings that I don't like start to appear in me, why do I envy the woman one next door? I think she steals his love ... luck smiles at her and she doesn't even turn to see me ... My joy has been erased, I have a sad face that I can't stand it, I've spent hours without eating, nothing appeals to me, well a carrot cupcake and a coffee does.

I am still faithful and I miss what the other gave me, even if it is little.

I dressed up and saw life in a different color, some little cute eyes winked at me and promised me the sky and the stars, I got on the wheel of fortune and came to a kind of jungle of incredible, fantastic treasures ... I was finally there happy.

I am a creature of habit, I returned to my routines, the party was over ...

At night I dream of my strong Adam, the one with the enchanted castle.

Against all reasoning my heart insists on pursuing him.

I told myself a thousand times that I could not bear to live for those who do not value me, but in my dreams he appears again ...

I arrived on Friday, my friends were looking for me for a meeting, they wanted me to give the introduction and recite my poems... I did not answer the phone, I was not at home, I wanted them not to take me into account, because I had other plans.

This love produces mixed feelings in me, the pain is present, but with my friends the joy is permanent ... even so I preferred to suffer.

Of course I would go, I listened to the song "if they leave us we will love each other" lost in my thoughts feeling like a heroine, a motorcyclist crossed my path and wrecked my car.

While talking to the insurance and complying with the protocols, time ran out, the appointment was kept in suspense.

I analyzed the options and in order not to mourn my misfortune, I gave my friends a surprise visit, I was filled with joy to feel so important, they kept looking for me and when I appeared they hugged me. For one night I was simple again, without complications ...

How long will it take to control my emotions well and not look for my elusive Adam? ...

It seems that God does not want me to go. The universe conspires and offers me other options ...

An ordinary day, another weekend alone ... What to do? I'll go find my insatiable lover ... I look for his touch and affection, my money pays for it , sometimes he gives me a smile, so weak that I can hardly make me be happy for 10 seconds, but I'm still in love with his unique way of loving me.

His house attracts me, when I walk away I only think of HIM. Stepping on the red carpet, imagining myself in Paris and that waltz melody transports me to the city of light.

I spend my time surrendered to the enchantment and when night falls I surrender to his sad love and I end up crying... alone without him.

In the moonlight I can see his silhouette, tall, strong, with semi-long hair marked by an Indian headband, but there is a detail wearing huaraches... No! it can't be him.

I remember him so elegant, distinguished, but I see him so little that I get confused ... The waitress looks like him ... I take the opportunity to ask about the owner, about my beloved, but she is silent and I do not get her out of her silence ... How strange is everything or will I be the strange one?

I know his there, why is he hiding?

He does not look at me, he does not touch me, he becomes a shadow, he is ungraspable, but I remain faithful chasing an illusion, tomorrow in the sunlight I know that I will look for him again.

It seems that I like to suffer that I like to lose ...

I went back to looking for him, blaming myself for being so weak... and I'm not in love, I'm passionate.

This Indian love brings out the worst in me ... jealousy, doubts, envy, selfishness ... I went to church to repent of my sin of loving someone who is not worth it ... it is not ME ... I do not know myself. Now I am cold, not very compassionate even greedy ... I don't spend on anything, I keep everything for HIM.

I have understood the dissatisfaction, sadness, loneliness and what hurts the most is his indifference.

I took refuge in the church, where nobody knows me, in this place my devotion grows and my faith puts me to the test ... I repent of my sins, I like to hear the Gospel from the lips of a colored priest who does not pronounce well and accentuates the words differently.

It seems that I am committed to change, not to look for what hurts me again.

The effect lasts a few hours, a few days at the most and I return to the beloved place.

The addiction is strong, it seems that the world stops in the people that we are about to leave it to tell us it is your time. You still have time and there with crutches, with oxygen masks, in wheelchairs I saw many Evas, some with their Adam and most of them alone, looking for the Indian to give us a caress.

The reality during the day was not so terrible, it is more inside the castle it was always daytime but you had to go out to everyone's life, and drive home. The road looked grotesque as a snake that could turn on you at any moment and it was raining... It was raining so much that you couldn't make out the lights of the city. Wrapped in that labyrinth, I was claiming to lose my security for an ungraspable being, an Indian love of legend.

MY LOVE – THE APACHE CASINO

I didn't want to be the fool looking for a love that took everything away and gave nothing so I left the Indian, my enchanted place and the Casino that had bewitched me.
The love of money never filled my life I didn't have to now.
I went back to searching after all love is a "search, find, search" formula.
I don't know where I read it, I remembered that when I had nowhere to go I took refuge in the yellowed pages of my books ... I returned to my silent lovers who comforted me without touching me, who made me cry with their tenderness and enchant me with their stories.
I was young again, the heroine of the story, the girl in the pink novel and even the evil one who made me cry to get so much rejection.
Loneliness seeks to reunite other loneliness and the lonely people and the loving ones also exist.
You had to look for a soul mate, even if it was at the end of the world, in an exotic place.
In a most unlikely place, on an island, he would find a castaway like me.
I found him... a different Adam with a physique that impressed me and an intelligence that impressed me even more. He didn't know how to smile ... he knew he was ugly and he walked away.
Well nothing is perfect, only love, but to receive it you have to feel worthy of deserving it and he believed that no one could love him. I did, but my interest seemed to humiliate him, he believed it was a pity and in me it was admiration. We do not function ... back to the routine of looking for another being, another Adam.

And there he was ... without looking for him I came to his life and his soul and my soul seemed to have been waiting forever, it could be said that each of his words were an echo of mine.

I knew that being in love is "Finding in a voice, one's own voice, deeply repeated."

I think that as in The Little Prince, you can love from a distance, be faithful to a flower that remained in another world, in another time and even if you see a garden full of them, your flower is irreplaceable, it is unique because it is the one you love.

Yes! This Adam is unique, of a wonderful simplicity, I don't need to have his body to love him.

Copulating in the dimension of the spirit is fullness, it is peace ... A transcendent love, sublime because it elevates you to unknown and magical skies.

At last. I am finally happy, although I know that with this love that nothing prevents, because it did not touch their routines or violated their spaces, time will be our enemy.

I will continue ... I will inform you. And if I don't have minutes left to live it, I'll ask time to come back.

I'm afraid of the crazy Adams but I know one, I close my door, I don't want to reject him but I have to do it in self-defense ... he doesn't know how to relate to anyone, he grew up as a small animal like a wild plant that nobody paid attention to.

Always rejected ... he lived on the street, he survived by a miracle and something that tells my heart that he is worthy of tenderness is his quiet pain and his brilliant intelligence.

He was educated by the goodness of the educational system and the intuition that an old teacher had who saw in him a diamond in the rough, a different being ... He was so original that he seemed not to have been born from the womb of a woman, but from the very bottom of the earth, like those seeds that sprout between stones with everything against it, but there they are. Some tear them up without giving them the opportunity to grow, but I already told you that he survived adversity.

His imagination is so rich because he knows all the worlds, he does not struggle to describe the most abject, the most absurd he was already there. You guessed it? He is a writer...

Our work as teachers brought us closer, although if I'm honest I tried to keep him far away. It seemed to me that his lack of affection led him to place his hands on all the waists, shoulders and buttocks of women. Some of them withdrew from him abruptly, I think so much rejection made him obsessive about sex.

I like what he writes, once I was touched by this crazy Adam and I was kind and I opened the doors of my library and invited my friends to read and listen to him.

We cried with his stories, we made him happy by buying his books. Again I prefer virtual reality to read it ... because in the real dimension I cannot give him what he is looking for. So the crazy Adam is banned, I will not remove the locks, I do not want to run into HIM.

I have no sweet memories with this character since he is bitter ... I will only remember how good I felt and made him feel by recognizing the merits that he has as a writer.

But... and if I don't find any more Adams, will Eva die of sadness?... We must love or hate... But... if neither love nor hate make us scream, then we are dead.

Keep looking Eva, keep looking ... I found him on the news, he doesn't remember me, but I do.

When he didn't have gray hair, when he was so agile he left everyone behind. He had a dream to become very important, so important that he would make our worn and ravaged space a land of promise.

I liked his ideas and helped him to spread them to win followers for his political party.

A party in which they never agreed and that was forged their near disappearance.

Talking about political parties does not work, it is not romantic, it is not beautiful, pure litigation and struggle of egos ...

Well my admired Adam is in fashion, he struggled too much to make a name for himself by getting out of the pieces of the party and forming a whole one for himself. He did it, he controlled, he met, he walked, he wore his shoes and he is about to occupy the chair that everyone wants.

Yes! but he has a lot of gray hair, he talks and walks slowly ... I already want to see him from his throne and see that power changes men ... What if not? What if he remembers me? of this millennial Eva who still believes in fairy tales and who is waiting for the prince to come and rescue her.

I wish for my prince to arrive and then maybe I'll go greet him. But this is a fantasy that is more forbidden than the apple of Eden, many snakes will be surrounding him, inviting him to the richest pleasures ... Do not believe my admired Adam, you cannot wear yourself out in worldly things ... Be careful of your own shadow, all the wealth in the world at your feet and your defenseless with so many thieves by your side.

I suffer for you and you will no longer have a life of your own, even your memories will be stolen and I live there.

I am that simple Eva with ideals similar to yours but I will no longer be able to speak to you. You came to a pedestal where touching yourself is impossible and thinking that you said that I was important ... now I'm just a sad and distant Eva that you have no memory of ...

Destiny you have not marked the final route for me ... is my admired Adam in it?

I answer myself, of course he will be there, but from afar in the magazines, on television screens, I even fear turning it on. Because it makes me uneasy and I start to wonder ... Will it hold up? Like he looks more tired, like he's older, like something hurts ... I read his interviews and they didn't ask him the questions I want to have answers for. Sometimes I would like to be closer, like a fly found in the most intimate corners and know that he is happy ... Not only Eva prays that this is the case. There are millions of Eves and Adams that we depend on his actions ... Let not anger tempt him because he will shake heads, let him not be a prisoner of revenge because it would break his soul, he must take advantage of the time to rule and what if he does not leave? I suffer again this novel is making me nervous.

Why would I like men of power so much? It is not my style to ask, everyone has given me, some more than I deserve, I have never needed anyone to live.

The only thing I will ask of the enthroned Adam is peace. I think he says love and peace for all. So be it...

I will return to the common Adam who does not have a penny, who I can take by the hand to put me in touch with reality, remove the cobwebs from my head and shake my dreams.

So much walking has made me tired. I'm not crazy I assure you ... Or am I?

EPILOGUE

The only Adam who has never disappointed me or will never disappoint me because he can no longer do it is my logical Adam... with him I learned that life is not about laughing all the time.
I was so free of thought and action with my Logical Adam that I chose lovers who would not bother him, books! They fill in my spaces, I sleep and wake up with them, they allow me to dream, travel, LIVE.
I will not look for more Adams...

www.ingramcontent.com/pod-product-compliance
Lightning Source LLC
LaVergne TN
LVHW040159080526
838202LV00042B/3228